PIERCE

ENCYCLOPEDIA
of PRESIDENTS

Franklin Pierce

Fourteenth President of the United States

By Charnan Simon

Consultant: Charles Abele, Ph.D.
Social Studies Instructor
Chicago Public School System

CHILDRENS PRESS ®

CHICAGO

President Pierce at a White House reception

Library of Congress Cataloging-in-Publication Data

Simon, Charnan.
 Franklin Pierce / by Charnan Simon.
  p.   cm. — (Encyclopedia of presidents)
 Includes index.
 Summary: Examines the life of the New Hampshire politician
who became the fourteenth president of the United States and
fought for strong states' rights and less federal authority.
 ISBN 0-516-01357-2
 1. Pierce, Franklin, 1804-1869—Juvenile
literature. 2. United States—Politics and government—
1853-1857—Juvenile literature. 3. Presidents—United
States—Biography—Juvenile literature. [1. Pierce,
Franklin, 1804-1869. 2. Presidents.] I. Title.
II. Series.
E432.S56   1988   88-10883
[92]—dc19   CIP
                                                        AC

Childrens Press®, Chicago

Picture Acknowledgments

The Bettmann Archive—4, 22, 26, 28, 31, 40,
41, 76, 79, 81, 87, 89

Historical Pictures Service, Chicago—5, 6, 8, 10,
11, 13, 16, 23, 24, 25, 29, 32, 35 (2 pictures), 37
(bottom), 38, 39, 42, 43, 46, 48, 49, 50, 51, 53,
54, 59 (3 pictures), 60, 62, 63 (2 pictures), 66,
67, 68, 69, 70, 73, 80

Courtesy Library of Congress—19 (bottom), 37
(top), 55, 56, 74, 85 (top)

National Portrait Gallery, Smithsonian
Institution—85 (bottom)

New Hampshire Historical Society—21, 45, 61,
65, 82, 88

North Wind Picture Archives—12, 18 (bottom),
19 (2 top pictures)

Sophia Smith Collection, Smith College—58, 78

Courtesy U.S. Bureau of Printing and
Engraving—2, 15, 18 (top)

Vision Quest—52

Cover design and illustration
by Steven Gaston Dobson

Two sides of a medal
commemorating the inauguration
of Franklin Pierce in 1853

Table of Contents

Chapter 1

A Chilly Day in March

March 4, 1853, dawned blustery and cold in Washington, D.C. But despite the biting northeasterly wind and the gusting snow, the streets were crowded with spectators. For days, politicians, tourists, and ordinary, interested citizens had been pouring into the nation's capital. They came by foot, on horseback, and by carriage. They packed the Potomac with steamboats, dinghies, and flatboats. By midmorning, more than seventy thousand people had gathered to jam Lafayette Square, line Pennsylvania Avenue, and swarm around the Capitol.

By noon the skies had cleared somewhat, and a pale sun was beginning to shine. As the clock struck twelve, the crowds grew momentarily silent. Drums rolled and brass bands struck up a triumphal march. A grand procession of militia, fire companies, and political clubs joined the carriage bearing outgoing President Millard Fillmore and President-Elect Franklin Pierce.

The procession continued to the Capitol for the inaugural ceremony. There in the Senate chamber, before the Congress, the Supreme Court, and the diplomatic corps, Franklin Pierce was sworn in as the fourteenth president of the United States.

Opposite page: President Franklin Pierce

Disappointed candidates congratulating Pierce on his nomination for president

It was a sobering moment for "Young Hickory," as Franklin Pierce was known. He hadn't actively campaigned for the presidency. As a young man, he had served as both a congressman and a senator. But since resigning from the Senate in 1842, he had considered his life as a public servant over. When the Democratic party held its nominating convention in June 1852, the party had no clear favorite to put up for nomination. After forty-nine ballots, support for the leading contenders—James Buchanan, Lewis Cass, Stephen Douglas, and William Marcy—had crumbled. A "dark-horse" compromise candidate, the personable but relatively inexperienced Franklin Pierce, had swept the field. From there it was a short step to defeating the Whig candidate, General Winfield Scott, and sweeping the national election.

His oath of office completed, Pierce stepped forward to deliver his inaugural address. At forty-eight, he was the youngest man thus far elected as president of the United States. And when he pushed aside his prepared notes and began speaking directly to the crowd, he became the first president to deliver his inaugural speech entirely from memory. But though the skies outside may have cleared, the forecast for Pierce's personal and political life was anything but sunny.

The cloud shadowing Pierce's personal life was obvious enough. Just two months before, on January 6, 1853, his third and last surviving child had been killed in a railway accident. Pierce's wife, Jane, felt that the tragic accident was a penalty for his accepting the presidency. She sank into a severe depression after the boy's death and was unable even to attend her husband's inauguration. It was to this private grief that Pierce referred in the opening lines of his speech:

"It is a relief to feel that no heart but my own can know the personal regret and bitter sorrow out of which I have been borne to a position so suitable for others rather than desirable for myself."

The cloud hanging over Pierce's political life was, perhaps, not quite so obvious, but it would prove to be even more devastating to his presidency. It wasn't a new trouble—it had haunted the nation since its birth sixty-four years earlier. But now the issue was growing ever more urgent. Until the question of slavery could be resolved once and for all, neither Pierce nor his country would know any real peace.

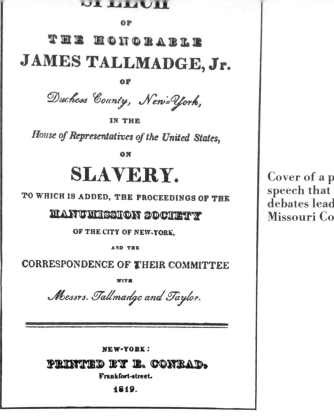

SPEECH
OF
THE HONORABLE
JAMES TALLMADGE, Jr.
OF
Duchess County, New-York,
IN THE
House of Representatives of the United States,
ON
SLAVERY.
TO WHICH IS ADDED, THE PROCEEDINGS OF THE
MANUMISSION SOCIETY
OF THE CITY OF NEW-YORK,
AND THE
CORRESPONDENCE OF THEIR COMMITTEE
WITH
Messrs. Tallmadge and Taylor.

NEW-YORK:
PRINTED BY E. CONRAD,
Frankfort-street.
1819.

Cover of a published speech that started the debates leading to the Missouri Compromise

When America was first settled, there had been slavery in all thirteen of the original colonies. But gradually slavery had died out in the North. The land there simply wasn't suited to the large, one-crop farms that could best benefit from slave labor.

As long as there were roughly as many slave states as free states, the balance of power between North and South remained equal. This was where matters stood in 1818, when the Union consisted of eleven free states and eleven slave states. But a bitter debate arose in 1819, when Missouri asked to be admitted as a slave state. This was more a political and economic debate than a moral one. The question was not whether slavery was good for the slaves themselves. Most Americans, both northerners and southerners, felt that the black slaves would never be fit to be citizens. No, the question was more about balance of

An 1849 cartoon entitled "The Scramble to Get to California"

power. The North wanted to halt the spread of slavery by outlawing it in the new states. The South wanted to preserve their power in the Senate by allowing one new slave state for every free state admitted to the Union.

After a long struggle in Congress, the Missouri Compromise was enacted in 1820. This law admitted Missouri as a slave state and Maine as a free state. The law also banned slavery in any future new states that lay north of the 36°30′ latitude, Missouri's southern border.

This uneasy truce between North and South held until 1850, when California petitioned for statehood. More than eighty thousand people had swarmed into California during the Gold Rush of 1849. Now they had drawn up a constitution and were ready to be admitted to the Union. And even though much of California lay south of the 36°30′ line, the people there firmly wished to enter as a free state.

Slaves working a cotton plantation

If hammering out a compromise in 1820 had been difficult, it was twice as hard in 1850. By now, many Americans in the North had come to see slavery as morally wrong. These people, known as abolitionists, wanted to abolish all slavery, in old states as well as new. The South, seeing their plantation economy threatened, fought the abolitionist movement fiercely.

The debate over slavery raged in Congress. Finally, after months of arguing, a set of laws was passed that was meant to satisfy both sides. These laws, known as the Compromise of 1850, allowed California to enter as a free state. To appease the South, Congress also created the territories

The Defendant in this case, one, Webster, a very Intellectual looking man, & was possessed of competence, which made the case appear more singular) was charged by the complainant (one Clay) with having purloined from his "Clays" pocket while he Clay was enjoying a long "Nap". (The Senator from Mississippi not having finished his speech) an important Paper, which the aforesaid Clay had been at much pains to procure for his own exclusive benefit, The Defendant "Webster" maintained a dogged Silence on the subject of the Theft but talked loudly about his "Constitutional rights" as an American Citizen. the strangest part of it was that as the Court room" the Defendant "Webster" was loudly applauded while the Complainant Clay was scarcely noticed.

Daniel Webster (left) debating with Henry Clay over the Compromise of 1850

of New Mexico and Utah, declaring that when these territories became states, they could decide on slavery for themselves. As another concession to the South, Congress established the Fugitive Slave Law, which made the federal government responsible for hunting down runaway slaves and returning them to their owners. It also outlawed the slave trade in Washington, D.C.

Thus another uneasy truce was struck. But the Compromise of 1850 did not stop the abolitionist movement. If anything, the harshness of the Fugitive Slave Law horrified many northerners and swelled the ranks of abolitionists. Southerners now recognized that the battle for slavery was, in fact, a battle for their very way of life.

This was the dark cloud overshadowing Pierce's presidential inauguration. As he stood before his fellow citizens that raw March day, he was well aware of the bitter issue that threatened to divide the Union. Though his speech touched boldly on the themes of territorial and trade expansion, he reserved his strongest arguments for the theme of slavery. He spelled out his support of slavery and of the Compromise of 1850 (including the Fugitive Slave Law) in no uncertain terms: "I believe that involuntary servitude, as it exists in different States of this Confederacy, is recognized by the Constitution. . . . I hold that the laws of 1850, commonly called the 'compromise measure,' are strictly constitutional and to be unhesitatingly carried into effect."

Pierce also made it clear that his beliefs were based on his firm convictions about states' rights. In this he proved himself deserving of the nickname "Young Hickory." Andrew Jackson, who had served as the country's seventh president from 1829 to 1837, was the original "Old Hickory." His policy of conservative management and strong states' rights came to be known as Jacksonian Democracy. Pierce had served as a junior congressman under him, and he strongly supported Jackson's policies. In fact, there were those who felt that Pierce "out-Jacksoned Jackson" in his fervent belief that the federal government's powers should be limited.

Pierce expressed this belief in his inaugural address when he stated: "If the Federal Government will confine itself to the exercise of powers clearly granted by the Constitution, it can hardly happen that its action upon any

Andrew Jackson

question should endanger the institutions of the States or interfere with their right to manage matters strictly domestic according to the will of their own people."

And so Franklin Pierce became president of the United States. His soothing conviction that simply abiding by the Constitution would put slavery questions to rest was soon shattered. As history would show, those questions would never be put to rest peacefully. The issue of slavery would not be resolved until the Civil War, only eight years away. And Franklin Pierce's political life would be one of the first casualties of that great and horrible war.

All in all, March 4, 1853, was a chilly day for President-Elect Franklin Pierce.

Concord, New Hampshire, the capital of Pierce's home state

Chapter 2

A New Hampshire Boyhood

The year 1804 was an exciting time for citizens of the United States. Thomas Jefferson had just begun his second term as president. The year before, he had doubled the size of the new republic by purchasing 827,987 square miles of land from France. This land, which stretched from the Mississippi River to the Rocky Mountains, was known as the Louisiana Purchase.

Now, in 1804, Jefferson had sent Meriwether Lewis and William Clark to explore this uncharted territory. The reports sent back from Lewis and Clark's expedition contained valuable information about the natural wealth of the West. They paved the way for thousands of hunters, traders, and pioneer families who would soon stream westward to settle these new lands.

There were now seventeen states in the Union. To the original thirteen had been added Vermont, Kentucky, Tennessee, and Ohio. But the Union was still young, and most of its citizens were farmers. In fact, much of Thomas Jefferson's political philosophy, which became known as Jeffersonian Democracy, was based on the ideal of America as a nation of small farmers. Jefferson felt that people should live simple, self-directed lives, and that there should be no need for a powerful federal government.

Left: Thomas Jefferson, who was responsible for the Louisiana Purchase

Below: A map showing the expansion of the United States through various treaties

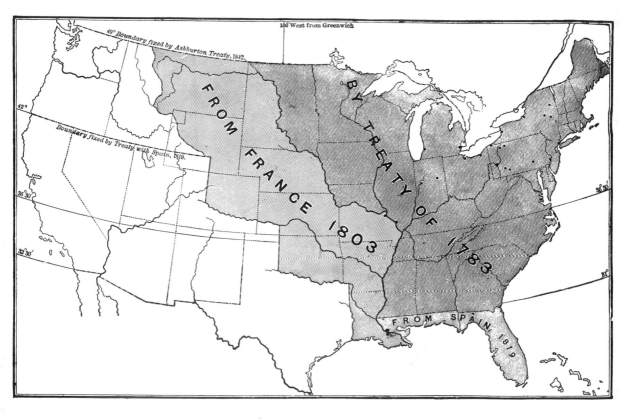

Above: Explorers William Clark (left) and Meriwether Lewis (right)
Below: Lewis and Clark meeting with Indians during their expedition

One farmer who certainly agreed with Jefferson was Benjamin Pierce, of Hillsborough, New Hampshire. Pierce came of old New England stock. His first American ancestor had settled in Charlestown, Massachusetts (today a part of Boston) in 1634. Benjamin had been only eighteen on April 19, 1775, when Paul Revere came galloping past the uncle's farm where he lived. Benjamin didn't hesitate when he heard the message that the British were coming. He unhitched his plow, picked up his gun and powder horn, and set out to fight the American Revolution.

Benjamin fought bravely for the next five years, serving at Ticonderoga, Fort Stanwix, and Valley Forge. General George Washington singled him out as one of his most valuable officers. When the war ended, Pierce settled on a farm in Hillsborough, New Hampshire. Here he continued his service to his country. Besides running the farm, Pierce served as city councilman, sheriff, and brigadier general of the state militia. Throughout it all, he held firmly to the ideals of Jefferson's Democratic-Republican party. Unlike Federalists George Washington, John Adams, and Alexander Hamilton, Jefferson's followers believed in strong states' rights and less federal authority.

Benjamin Pierce would pass these beliefs on to his eight children—particularly to his son Franklin, who would someday be the country's fourteenth president. All his life, Franklin would prove himself a true son of his father. He would believe in military service as being a necessary part of public service. And he would strictly adhere to the idea that the federal government shouldn't interfere with the states' rights to manage their own affairs.

The Pierce homestead in Hillsborough, New Hampshire

Franklin Pierce grew up breathing politics. He was born on November 23, 1804, in a log cabin on his father's old homestead. Soon thereafter the family moved to a frame house in the main village of Hillsborough. This house was located on a highway and occasionally served as a tavern. Travelers from as far away as Concord — the state capital, six hours away by horse — often stopped by for refreshments or to spend the night. From them young Franklin heard all the news of the day.

But life wasn't all politics. Franklin spent most of his time outdoors, as did youngsters all over the country. He learned to fish and trap and to handle a gun at an early age. What he liked best was listening to his father's thrilling stories about the revolutionary war. A soldier in his country's service — that was the life for young Frank!

Francis Scott Key observing Fort McHenry from aboard ship

When he was just eight years old, the country was plunged into another war with Great Britain. Franklin's father went off to Concord as a member of the governor's advisory council during this War of 1812, while his mother and sisters continued to run the family tavern. All day long, a stream of soldiers passed along the turnpike in front of the Pierce house. They brought exciting stories of being in the militia and guarding the state from an invasion of hated Redcoats. They told of an American lawyer named Francis Scott Key, who, watching a British fleet pound Fort McHenry in 1814, scrawled the words for a stirring song on the back on an old envelope: "O say can you see by the dawn's early light What so proudly we hail'd, at the twilight's last gleaming . . . ? And the rocket's red glare, the bombs bursting in air, Gave proof through the night that our flag was still there. . . . "

Bowdoin College in
Brunswick, Maine

When Franklin's two older brothers went off to fight,
Franklin begged to go, too. But his mother was firm. She
sent him off, all right—to the little red brick schoolhouse
at Hillsborough Center! And when he'd learned all he
could there, his father sent him to boarding school at the
Hancock Academy.

The war ended, and Franklin was sent to Francestown
Academy to take the final courses he needed before col-
lege. His older brother had attended nearby Dartmouth
College, but now General Pierce felt that the school's
teachings leaned too heavily toward a Federalist point of
view. So in 1820 Franklin was sent to Bowdoin College in
Brunswick, Maine—which maintained good, Democratic-
Republican political views.

Bowdoin College students hold a fanciful parade through town.

Once at Bowdoin, Franklin studied Greek, Latin, and arithmetic. Rules were strict. Students couldn't "attend any theatrical entertainments or any idle show in Brunswick . . . nor play at cards, billiards, or any game of hazard . . . nor go shooting or fishing. . . . No student shall be concerned in loud and disorderly singing in College, in shouting or clapping hands. . . . Students must be in their rooms Saturday and Sunday evenings and abstain from diversions of every kind. . . ."

But despite the strictness, young Pierce managed to find time to enjoy himself. In fact, he found much more time for amusements and friends—including a shy young man named Nathaniel Hawthorne—than he did for studying. By the end of his sophomore year, he ranked at the very bottom of his class.

Author Nathaniel Hawthorne, who wrote a biography of Franklin Pierce

Shocked, Franklin decided to mend his ways. For the next two years he was a model scholar—chapel monitor, captain of the military company of students, chairman of the Athenean Literary Society. By the time he graduated in 1824, he had risen to fifth in his class and was selected to make a commencement speech. For the first—but certainly not the last—time in his life, Franklin Pierce had proved that when he decided to do a thing, he did it right!

The south front of the White House in 1825

Chapter 3

A First Taste of Politics

When Franklin Pierce graduated from Bowdoin College in the summer of 1824, the United States was brimming with good feeling. President James Monroe was well into his second term of office. The year before, he had issued his famous Monroe Doctrine, which warned Europeans against interfering in the affairs of North and South America. The Missouri Compromise of 1820 had ended a major slavery dispute between North and South—at least temporarily. Westward expansion had begun, with settlers pushing the frontier across the Mississippi River into Iowa, Missouri, Arkansas, and Texas. Travel now was easier than ever. Work on the Cumberland Road, from Maryland to Illinois, had begun in 1821 with funding from the federal government. And the Erie Canal, a 360-mile-long canal connecting Lake Erie with the Hudson River (and hence the Atlantic Ocean), was nearing completion, after eight years of backbreaking labor.

President John Quincy Adams

All in all, it was an exciting time for a young man in a burgeoning country, and Franklin Pierce lost no time getting into the thick of things. Since there was no war to be fought, he decided to set himself up for public life. With that in mind, he returned to Hillsborough. He took up the position of postmaster to support himself and began studying law with a local lawyer named John Burnham. This lasted only a year; by 1825, John Quincy Adams was elected president of the United States, and the job of postmaster had gone to someone with Federalist leanings.

Pierce's first law office in New Hampshire

Franklin then moved to Portsmouth and continued studying in the law offices of Levi Woodbury. Two years later, in 1827, he passed the bar exams and was admitted to practice law in New Hampshire—the same year his father was elected governor of the state.

Politics in the United States was heating up. On the one hand, there were the supporters of John Quincy Adams and his Federalist-like beliefs. On the other hand were the supporters of Andrew Jackson, a military hero from the War of 1812. Jackson appealed to the "common man." He promised to end what he termed the "monopoly" of government by the long-established, well-to-do families.

The Pierce family were staunch Jackson supporters. While Benjamin Pierce was serving as governor of New Hampshire, Franklin threw himself into local politics. In 1829 his hard work paid off. Andrew Jackson had been elected president of the United States, Benjamin Pierce had begun his second term as governor, and Franklin Pierce was elected to the New Hampshire legislature.

Young Pierce quickly learned that he liked politics. He was a lively speaker and a hard worker, and he soon made himself popular with the Jacksonian Democrats in Concord. (The name Democratic-Republican was gradually dropped, and the party eventually became the Democratic party of today.)

Franklin did have to guard against his tendency to overdo it with the rest of the rough-and-tumble, hard-drinking legislators. Nevertheless, he always kept his family reputation in mind and took his responsibilities as a legislator seriously.

Pierce's hard work paid off. He was returned to the legislature in 1830 and again in 1831, when he was nominated to be speaker of the House.

Franklin served honorably as speaker. A twenty-six-year-old politician, he was learning the ins and outs of practical politics as he presided over the 229 legislators. It was an experience that would stand him in good stead for the rest of his life.

The year 1832 was another banner year for the Pierce family. Andrew Jackson was handily renominated for president, and Franklin Pierce, an ardent Jacksonian, was returned to the legislature in Concord. Again he was elected speaker of the House—this time he was elected almost unanimously.

An additional honor came when he was named to a committee of five to draw up a list of candidates for state offices—from governor to U.S. congressman. But when the committee met, it was Franklin Pierce who became the congressional nominee.

Full-length portrait of President Andrew Jackson

Pierce campaigned throughout the summer for Jackson, traveling by horse and by carriage all over New Hampshire and Massachusetts. His father, meanwhile, had been selected a presidential elector and was off to Washington to cast his vote for the family favorite. When election time finally rolled around, both Jackson and Franklin Pierce were in office. It was time to move to Washington!

Chapter 4

On to Washington

Franklin Pierce meant to travel around the United States that spring of 1833, before settling into Washington for the fall session of Congress. But the winter before, Asian cholera had broken out in New York City, and now the dreaded disease had spread all over the eastern seaboard. In one twelve-day period, over six thousand people had died in New Orleans, and the scenario was nearly as bad in most other coastal cities. Pierce did visit his sister in Boston—and promptly contracted the disease. For weeks he hovered between life and death, but by fall was well enough to continue his trip to the nation's capital.

And what a trip it was! Two horse-drawn coaches, two steamboats, a jaunt on the New Amboy and Camden Railroad (at a record eighteen miles per hour!), two more steamboats, another railroad jaunt, another steamboat, and a final coach ride into Washington, D.C. It was no wonder that people in the mid-1800s didn't take cross-country travel lightly!

Once in Washington, Pierce quickly settled into one of the many boardinghouses where senators and congressmen lived. Few legislators bothered to own houses in Washington. With the congressional session running only from December to March, it was hardly worth the effort. Most of the men boarded in various houses around the city, leaving their wives and children at home to run the family farms and businesses. (Of course, there were no women in Congress in those days—women across the country didn't even get voting rights until 1920.)

That first year in Washington was a busy one for Pierce. He was appointed to the Judiciary Committee of the House of Representatives, which looked into such things as patent renewals and court claims. Pierce worked hard on his committee and loyally supported President Jackson. It was during this period that Pierce began to make a reputation for "out-Jacksoning Jackson." While he supported the president in his stand to abolish the national bank, he strayed from the party line in other respects. He voted against federal support for a variety of internal improvements, such as roads and canals, holding firm to the Jeffersonian principle that the federal government should never intrude on individual states' rights. "Let the states take care of such matters as internal improvements and the granting of lands," he said.

But the main issue before Congress that session was the national bank. After a fierce and often bitter debate, Jackson finally had his way and the national bank was eliminated. At the same time, a new anti-Jackson party, the Whigs, came to life.

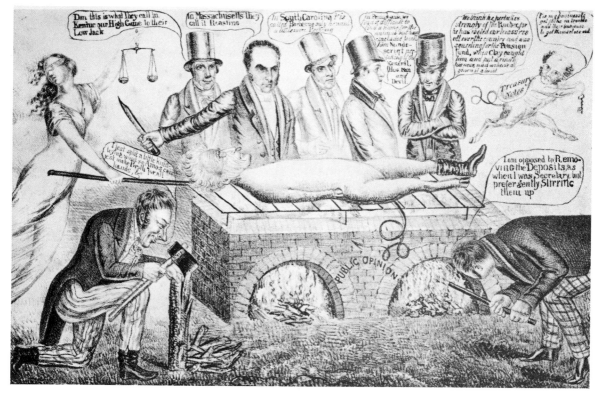

Above: Andrew Jackson
being roasted because
of the national bank
controversy

Right: An anti-Jackson
cartoon referring to
his hanging of two
Englishmen suspected
of aiding the Seminole
Indians during the
Seminole War in Florida

Neither Pierce nor the people of New Hampshire cared much about this new party. New Hampshire liked its junior congressman from Hillsborough, and he was readily reelected to Congress the next year.

But when Pierce returned to Washington in November 1834, he did not go alone. This time, he was accompanied by his new bride, Jane Means Appleton Pierce. The daughter of a former president of Bowdoin College, Jane was an aristocratic Whig. She was also a delicate girl who had refined tastes and was rumored to have tuberculosis.

The 1834 session was an unremarkable one for Pierce. He and Jane settled into their boardinghouse, and he introduced her to such social life as the rough-and-tumble capital offered. It wasn't much—certainly not to a girl who had grown up in Boston with its many cultural offerings, including the brand-new Boston Academy of Music.

When Congress adjourned on March 4, 1835, Franklin and Jane Pierce prepared to return home to Hillsborough. While Jane stopped in Boston for a visit with relatives, Franklin went on to New Hampshire to buy a house and begin refurbishing it. Jane joined him in May, and they spent the summer getting their house, farm, and law business in order.

This domestic tranquillity wasn't to last long, however. Once again Franklin was reelected to Congress, and when fall rolled around, he was off for Washington again. This time, however, it was decided that Jane would stay with her relatives in Boston. Traveling was difficult because of her delicate constitution, and the capital itself was just not quite civilized enough for her.

Right: Jane Pierce,
Franklin's wife

Below: Washington, D.C.,
as viewed from the
president's house, 1830

James Knox Polk

This term was a bit more exciting for Franklin Pierce. He was a third-time congressman, well-versed in the internal ways of his country's government. And he had for a friend James K. Polk of Tennessee, who was this year's Speaker of the House. Like Pierce, Polk was a staunch Jacksonian and a believer in states' rights. Unlike Pierce, he was a southerner and a slave owner. Through his friendship with Polk and other influential southerners, Pierce became more and more convinced that each state should decide the question of slavery for itself. In Pierce's view, it was not the federal government's place to interfere with the right of the people to govern themselves at the local level. Apparently, it never entered Pierce's mind that slavery might be a moral issue as well as a political one.

Senator John C. Calhoun

Because of his close personal friendship with Polk, Pierce was named to several special committees in 1835. He worked hard, but Congress itself was a house divided. The bitter quarrel between abolitionists and slaveholders was coming to a head. Pierce himself was drawn into the controversy in a debate with Senator John C. Calhoun of South Carolina. Calhoun had resigned as vice-president of the United States in 1832 to take up South Carolina's complaint against the tariffs of 1828 and 1832. He was firmly opposed to the idea that the Union could impose standards on individual states. Pierce, who had supported the tariffs, felt called upon to defend himself. He felt that Calhoun had misunderstood him and was, in effect, calling him a liar. During this debate Pierce's first child, Franklin, Jr., died only three days after birth. Worn out by personal sorrow and political disputes, Pierce fell ill with pleurisy.

A cartoon showing some of the ills plaguing the country in the mid-1800s

When he returned to Congress after his illness, he found chaos. Texas had won its rebellion against Mexico, and abolitionists feared the new territory would soon be petitioning for statehood as a slave state. Abolitionists stepped up their petitions to Congress, calling for a halt to slavery. Hoping to avoid the issue, the Senate established a system whereby the petitions were rejected without even being read. In the House, the petitions were halted by a "gag rule." This was clearly at odds with the First Amendment to the Constitution, which gives every citizen the

"The Disappointed Abolitionists" get a hostile reaction in this 1838 cartoon.

right to petition Congress for redressing wrongs. John Quincy Adams led an eloquent fight against this gag rule, but it would be eight years before he succeeded in abolishing it. In the meantime, an atmosphere that was half-carnival, half-battlefield reigned in the Congress of 1836. It was with a sense of weary relief that Pierce finally saw the end of the session and returned to New Hampshire.

The fall of 1836 saw Pierce back in Washington—this time with Jane, ill and unhappy from the loss of her baby, at his side. But Pierce was not reelected to the House this time. Instead, on March 4, 1837, he began serving a six-year term as United States senator. The citizens of New Hampshire had decided they needed Pierce for bigger things.

President
Martin
Van Buren

Being a senator did not have that many external advantages over being a congressman. The senators' desks were larger and more ornate, and their quill pens and paper were supplied fresh every day by pages. Four large fireplaces heated the Senate chamber, but that was about the extent of the comforts. As a sign in the visitors' gallery read, "You Are Requested Not to Put Your Feet Through the Railings, as The Dirt Falls on the Members' Heads."

Senator Pierce was primarily a committeeman under President Martin Van Buren, as he had been under President Jackson. As a speaker, he could not compare with such giants of his day as Henry Clay, John C. Calhoun, and Daniel Webster. He continued to believe that slavery was an issue best left for the South and the territories to resolve for themselves.

Senator Henry Clay

He also grew more determined in his opposition to the abolitionists and to the Whigs, whom he believed were using the slavery issue for their own political ends. These feelings came to a head when Pierce's friend and former college mate Jonathan Cilley, now a congressman from Maine, was killed in a duel. As Cilley's friend, Pierce had tried to stop the duel; when that failed, he reluctantly helped to make the arrangements for it. After the duel, Pierce came to believe that the whole thing had been arranged by Cilley's Whig enemies, who wanted to silence Cilley's opposition.

Disgusted by the affair, and by political life in general, the Pierces considered leaving the Senate behind and moving West. There, they felt, an honest man could still live an unsullied, independent life.

But the fall of 1838 found Franklin back in Washington. He continued to oppose any legislation that allowed the federal government to meddle in the states' rights and responsibilities. Roads, railroads, harbor improvements— let the states that needed them pay for them. It wasn't his responsibility, as a senator from New Hampshire, to vote money from the federal treasury for a railroad in Georgia.

In 1838 the Pierces moved from Hillsborough to the state capital of Concord. There Franklin would find more law opportunities when he left the Senate. Both Pierces were now actively looking forward to Franklin's retirement from public service. When Franklin returned to Washington in the fall of 1838, Jane stayed behind in the new house in Concord. She had a new son to care for— young Frank Robert Pierce.

Senator Pierce spent most of his time for the next two years doing routine committee work. But the pace picked up in 1840, when the Whig party challenged Pierce's Democrats in the national elections. Despite Pierce's strenuous campaigning for Martin Van Buren, Whig candidate William Henry Harrison was elected president of the United States. When he died a few weeks after catching a cold in his inaugural parade, Vice-President John Tyler took over.

This was the beginning of a difficult time for Franklin Pierce. For the first time since his arrival in Washington

The building where Franklin Pierce had a law office in Concord, New Hampshire

nine years earlier, he was a member of the minority party. This made things much more difficult for a senator — especially with such formidable opponents as Henry Clay and Daniel Webster.

Personally, things were not going well for the Pierces, either. Their finances had never really recovered from the depression of 1837, and they were deeply in debt. As if that weren't enough, young Frank died of typhus fever in 1841. Jane was even more despondent over his death than she had been over Franklin, Jr.'s five years earlier. With her strong encouragement, Franklin resigned from the Senate in 1842. It was time to return to Concord and take up life as a family man and a financially successful lawyer.

Chapter 5

Peace—and War

For the first few years, Franklin Pierce's retirement from public life went much as he expected. He established a thriving law practice and, largely at Jane's prodding, gave up drinking to conduct a temperance drive that left Concord a dry city.

But he didn't escape politics altogether. He was soon chairman of the state Democratic party and campaigned vigorously when his old friend, James Polk, was named the Democratic nominee for president in 1844. The Democratic party was becoming increasingly proslavery, believing that the slavery issue should be left to individual states. In trying to keep slavery out of national politics, Polk proved himself a typical Democrat. Like Pierce, Polk didn't talk much about whether slavery was right or wrong. His main concern was to absolve the federal government from responsibility in the issue. This would prove to be a hopeless stance in the long run—but for the time being it met with the approval of a sizable number of voters.

Opposite page: General Franklin Pierce

A great meeting in New York City in 1845 regarding Texas's statehood

At any rate, Pierce promised to produce ten thousand Democratic votes from New Hampshire — and he delivered them. Polk was so pleased by Pierce's campaign efforts that, after his election, he appointed Pierce federal district attorney for New Hampshire.

Pierce continued to speak out at town meetings on various Democratic issues. The other big issue of the day was Texas. Many voters in New Hampshire were opposed to slavery; they resisted the idea of bringing another slave state, as Texas was sure to be, into the Union. But as Pierce argued, if the United States didn't take Texas, Great Britain would. And that would change the shape of the North American continent permanently.

A romantic illustration of the idea of Manifest Destiny

By the mid-1840s, the United States had pushed its frontiers all the way to the Pacific Ocean. A disagreement with Britain over the Oregon Territory was resolved in 1846, when Britain ceded much of the disputed land to the U.S. Now Americans were looking south to additional lands from Mexico. In 1845, an editor named John L. O'Sullivan had written of "the fulfillment of our manifest destiny to overspread the continent allotted by Providence for the free development of our yearly multiplying millions." The doctrine of Manifest Destiny—that the United States should cover all of North America—was now eagerly embraced by a great many Americans.

General Winfield Scott entering Mexico City during the Mexican War

In the summer of 1846, President Polk offered Pierce a job in his cabinet, as United States Attorney General. Pierce refused the offer—as well as a proposed appointment to the Senate—for he now had other plans. The conflict with Mexico had come to a head. Polk had sent General Zachary Taylor to occupy disputed land near the Rio Grande River. Taylor's troops had clashed with Mexican soldiers, and on May 13, 1846, Congress had declared war on Mexico. Here at last was Pierce's chance to realize a lifelong ambition—to serve his country at war.

Pierce enlisted in the United States Army as a private. Soon he was appointed a colonel in the infantry and then given a commission as brigadier general. He and his men sailed for Vera Cruz, Mexico, on May 27, where General Winfield Scott was waiting for reinforcements.

American troops coming ashore at Vera Cruz

If Pierce had been expecting the Mexican War to cover him with military glory, he was sorely disappointed. He and his brigade of 2,500 men landed in the swampland of Vera Cruz on June 27, 1847, only to find that no one was there. Scott had moved on to Puebla, 150 miles away, and was waiting for Pierce's reinforcements. The 2,000 wild mules that had been assembled to pull their supply wagons were just that—wild. After breaking the mules until they were somewhat controllable, Pierce moved his men a few miles north of the city. There they made camp until a ship-load of horses arrived from New Orleans. On July 14, the brigade was on its way. The men and animals struggled in hot, humid weather, sometimes in waist-deep sand, lucky to make five miles a day. Finally they came to the Mexican national highway, which made its concrete way through lush, fertile plains and valleys.

General Winfield Scott

The brigade saw its first fighting on July 19, when it was ambushed by a detachment of Mexicans. Two days later the men took their first Mexican fort above the Antigua River. After several more skirmishes, they reached General Scott's army in Puebla, and on August 10, the combined forces of 11,000 set out for Mexico City.

Then came the first of several disappointing battles for Pierce. While fighting a large Mexican force near San Augustin on August 18, Pierce was knocked unconscious during the first few minutes of battle. Another officer, unaware of Pierce's condition, called out to Colonel Ransom to take charge: "Take command of the brigade, General Pierce is a damned coward."

When Pierce came to, he struggled on, despite a nasty knock on the head and a badly wrenched knee. But luck

Americans storming the fortress of Molino del Rey

was not with him that day. He twisted his injured knee again, and once more fell from the saddle. Though unable to fight, he nonetheless refused to be carried from the field. But without his active leadership, his men were unable to win the day.

Though General Scott commended Pierce's actions, he was destined not to fulfill his dream of becoming a military hero. In the next major battle, to capture the fortress of Molino del Rey, Pierce was put in charge of the reserve force—which wasn't needed to win the battle. Next, the Battle of Chapultepec found Pierce disabled by dysentery. Still, he roused himself for the last few minutes of the fighting—only to have the Mexican force surrender before he could lead a charge against them.

Loading a cannon at the Battle of Chapultepec

So Pierce returned to the United States, popular with most of his men and fellow officers, but certainly not covered with the cloak of glory. When the Mexican War was over, the United States had gained a broad stretch of territory from Texas to California—what is now the entire southwestern quarter of the United States. That, with the Oregon lands ceded from Great Britain, brought the total U.S. area to some three million square miles. The young nation was now nearly four times the size it had been when it gained its independence—almost as large as the whole of Europe. The Mexican War was a tremendous victory for the U.S. And Franklin Pierce, having to be satisfied with his small part in the victory, returned to Concord, determined that his life as a public servant was ended.

Opposite page: General Pierce in uniform

Chapter 6

The Presidency

By the mid-nineteenth century, the United States seemed to be in a golden age of prosperity. The country stretched from the Atlantic Ocean clear to the Pacific, and its population of over twenty-three million topped that of Great Britain. Immigrants were flooding the country from Ireland, Germany, The Netherlands, and Great Britain, attracted by the promise of vast, unclaimed lands, a democratic government—and California gold. Telegraph lines had been established between New York and Chicago, while railroads were rapidly expanding across the eastern part of the country. American cotton was prized around the world, and U.S. clipper ships were the fastest and most graceful on the seas.

Zachary Taylor was president, having been elected in 1848 almost solely on his record as a Mexican War hero. For once, the nation was glad to let the question of slavery take second place in a presidential election.

Harriet Beecher Stowe, author of *Uncle Tom's Cabin*

But underneath this prosperity the slavery issue still festered. The Underground Railroad, an escape route through which blacks were moved into free territory, was thriving. Harriet Beecher Stowe's book *Uncle Tom's Cabin*, which portrayed in graphic details the miseries of slavery, incensed antislavery northerners. Tempers were rising over whether or not California should be admitted as a free state. Outright hostilities were perhaps prevented only by Daniel Webster's impassioned speech of March 7, 1850. His plea was largely responsible for pushing through resolutions that scttlcd thc California question and established the Fugitive Slave Law. Known as the Compromise of 1850, these measures held off the catastrophe of civil war for ten more years.

UNCLE TOM'S CABIN;

OR,

LIFE AMONG THE LOWLY.

BY

HARRIET BEECHER STOWE.

VOL. I.

BOSTON:
JOHN P. JEWETT & COMPANY.
CLEVELAND, OHIO:
JEWETT, PROCTOR & WORTHINGTON.
1852.

Right: The cover of an early edition of *Uncle Tom's Cabin*

Below left: Poster announcing a reward for a fugitive slave

Below right: An 1851 poster warning blacks to look out for people who may try to capture them as fugitives

$200 REWARD!

Ran away from his owner [a Lady residing near Upper Marlboro, Prince George's County, Md.] on or about the 12th inst. of this month, a bright Mullatto man named Frank, a carpenter by trade, he is about five feet 9 or 10 inches high, light grey eyes, slow in speech, and very good personal appearance, about twenty-five years of age, his clothing good.

One Hundred dollars will be paid if apprehended within thirty miles of home, if more than thirty, the above reward, provided he be secured in Jail so that his owner gets him again.

W. D. BOWIE,

for the owner,

Buena Vista Post Office, Prince George's Co. Md.
February 14th, 1853.

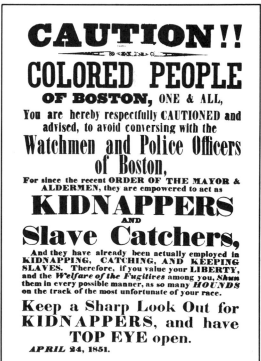

CAUTION!!

COLORED PEOPLE

OF BOSTON, ONE & ALL,

You are hereby respectfully CAUTIONED and advised, to avoid conversing with the

Watchmen and Police Officers of Boston,

For since the recent ORDER OF THE MAYOR & ALDERMEN, they are empowered to act as

KIDNAPPERS

AND

Slave Catchers,

And they have already been actually employed in KIDNAPPING, CATCHING, AND KEEPING SLAVES. Therefore, if you value your LIBERTY, and the *Welfare of the Fugitives* among you, *Shun* them in every possible manner, as so many *HOUNDS* on the track of the most unfortunate of your race.

Keep a Sharp Look Out for KIDNAPPERS, and have TOP EYE open.

APRIL 24, 1851.

Henry Clay addresses the Senate during the Compromise of 1850 debates.

The Compromise of 1850 also marked the beginning of the end of the Whig party, which sponsored the resolutions. Southerners saw the Whigs as soft on slavery, while northern voters viewed them with distaste because of the Fugitive Slave Law. Even within the party there was dissension. When the Whigs met on June 16, 1852, for their presidential nominating convention, it took fifty-three ballots before they could agree on a candidate. Their choice? General Winfield Scott, another Mexican War hero. If Zachary Taylor could get elected on the basis of military glory, perhaps Scott could, too.

And what of the Democrats during this time? Even with the Compromise of 1850, the country was sharply divided on the issue of slavery. A compromise candidate—one who wasn't well known enough to be disliked—was called for. That's where Franklin Pierce came in.

The Democrats' presidential campaign banner

Since the Mexican War, Pierce had been living quietly in New Hampshire. He spent his time pursuing an extremely successful law practice and stumping for Democratic measures throughout the state. But though he was widely known and admired in his own home state, he was still largely a blank to the rest of the nation. It had been ten years since he had served in the Senate, and even then he had not been well known nationally. If he had no staunch admirers in the South and the West, he at least had no enemies, either. On the forty-ninth ballot, Franklin Pierce was named the Democratic nominee for president.

A pro-Scott campaign cartoon, showing him taking the presidential seat from Pierce

Pierce and his wife were in Boston when the news of his nomination reached them. Jane, who had hated Washington ten years earlier and who felt politics was an unclean occupation, promptly fainted when she heard the news. She had been happy these last ten years. She enjoyed living in Concord and raising their third and only surviving son, Benjamin, born in 1841. Now it seemed those happy years were coming to an end.

And so they were, in many ways. On November 2, 1852, Franklin Pierce won the presidential election. He was a majority president, but just barely. To his 1,600,000 votes, General Scott had pulled 1,385,000 — yet another indication of how sharply divided the Union really was.

More political cartoons issued during the 1852 presidential campaign

Then, before the Pierces even reached Washington for the inauguration, a tragic train accident claimed twelve-year-old Benjamin's life on January 6, 1853. Jane Pierce broke down completely after the accident. The foreboding she had felt about Franklin's accepting the presidency had come true. It would be months before she was well enough to travel to Washington. Even then, she would never take up her position as White House hostess. Throughout the Pierce administration, that role would be filled by Jane's friend and distant relative, Abigail Kent Means. Throughout his presidency, Franklin Pierce would be emotionally distracted by his own family tragedy and would blame himself for the sorry state of his wife's health.

Franklin Pierce would not only be without a wife at his side during his inauguration. His vice-president, William Rufus Devane King, lay ill in Cuba that chilly March day in 1853. A special act of Congress allowed him to take his oath of office there, but he died on April 18, having served as vice-president only six weeks. For the remainder of his term, Pierce would serve without a vice-president.

Thus it was with a heavy heart that Franklin Pierce began his term as fourteenth president of the United States. First on the agenda was to select a cabinet. Well aware of the discord that split the nation, Pierce looked to balance his cabinet. Carefully he chose a coalition of southern planters and northern businessmen. It was an odd mixture of men, but it turned out to be the only cabinet in American history to survive a president's term without a change.

Opposite page: Jane Pierce and son Benjamin

James Gadsden

Then it was down to business. As he had promised in his inaugural address, Pierce pursued an aggressive foreign policy. The border between the United States and Mexico was still vague, and Mexico was occupying land that America also claimed. Pierce's secretary of war, Jefferson Davis of Mississippi, wanted those lands for a proposed transcontinental railroad that would benefit the southern states. Urged on by Davis, Pierce sent a railroad man, James Gadsden, to buy the disputed land. On April 24, 1854, the Gadsden Purchase fixed the Mexican border at its current location. This proved to be the final enlargement of United States territory on this continent.

Practical-minded thugs carry out the principle of the Ostend Manifesto on James Buchanan.

Pierce had less success with his plans to acquire Cuba. He instructed three of his European ministers—Pierre Soule in Spain, James Buchanan in Great Britain, and John Mason in France—to meet in Ostend, Belgium, on October 9, 1854, to discuss the matter of Cuba. The ministers decided that the United States should offer Spain $120 million for the purchase of Cuba. If Spain did not accept, the U.S. would be justified in going to war over the island. It was a disastrous decision. When word of the conference leaked to the press, it stirred up an international storm of dissent. The United States was forced to issue a disclaimer about the "Ostend Manifesto," and all hope of buying Cuba was abandoned.

Perry's first landing in Japan in 1853

Things went more smoothly for Pierce in the Far East. For nearly three hundred years, Japan had held fast to its policy of isolationism, refusing to admit Western diplomats and traders. Now the United States wanted Japanese ports opened to Yankee clipper ships trading in China, as well as to American whalers in the north Pacific. Pierce authorized Commodore Matthew C. Perry to take a U.S. naval fleet into Tokyo Harbor in July 1853. In February 1854 he followed up with a second fleet, suitably loaded up with such examples of advanced Western civilization as

Perry pays his farewell visit to Japanese officials after concluding a trade treaty.

guns, telegraphs, telescopes, and model railroads. The Japanese were properly impressed, and on March 31, 1854, a treaty inaugurating U.S. diplomatic and trade relations with Japan was signed.

Throughout Pierce's term as president, however, foreign expansion was to take a back seat to more pressing domestic problems. He took every opportunity to define slavery as a state issue and not a federal one. But Pierce was soon forced to deal head-on with the question which, more than any other in our nation's history, had the power to tear the Union apart.

Chapter 7

Kansas and Nebraska

All was not well in the White House. While Pierce struggled to appoint a cabinet and get on with the business of government, Jane sank into a deeper and deeper depression. She let others handle the details of public and private functions, spending her time thinking about her lost son and writing him sad, loving letters.

If Pierce's personal life was in disarray, his political life was about to become even more disorderly. He had vowed to keep the federal government out of the slavery issue. But Pierce soon found the two parts of the nation—slave and free—on a collision course. It was a crisis his administration could not ignore.

The trouble centered around U.S. lands that had not yet been organized into official territories. These lands ranged roughly between Missouri and present-day Idaho. It was prime settling land; it was also prime land for the proposed transcontinental railway—or so thought Senator Stephen A. Douglas of Illinois. Douglas had invested a lot of money in railroads, and he wasn't pleased to see railroad interests directed south. So in 1854 he introduced a bill to organize the Nebraska Territory.

The proposal caused trouble right from the start. Southern senators insisted that the people in the new territory should be allowed to decide for themselves whether or not to permit slavery. This was directly contrary to what had been established in the Missouri Compromise of 1820. The compromise provided that slavery would be "forever prohibited" in all the Louisiana Purchase territory north of the 36°30′ line, Missouri's southern boundary.

Douglas, who had presidential ambitions, saw that he would have to placate the South. So he modified his bill. Instead of one territory, he suggested, there should be two—Kansas and Nebraska. The people in each should be allowed to determine for themselves whether or not to permit slavery. Douglas felt this would appease the South. To placate the North, Douglas assured Congress that he wasn't overthrowing the Missouri Compromise. He claimed he was just following the policies of the later Compromise of 1850, which left the question of slavery in the territories up to the settlers living there.

But this wasn't enough for some southern senators. They demanded an outright repeal of the Missouri Compromise. Douglas finally agreed to this, and he and Jefferson Davis set about bringing President Pierce around to their way of thinking. Douglas supporters even threatened to block Pierce's appointees and veto the Gadsden Purchase if he didn't support the Kansas-Nebraska bill.

Unfortunately, Pierce felt he had no choice but to go along with Douglas and his supporters. He endorsed the Kansas-Nebraska bill, and the federal government was back in the slavery fray.

Kansas abolitionists breaking up a camp of invading proslavery people

Three months of bitter debate followed, with Pierce harshly criticized by northern and abolitionist newspapers. The bill was finally—and narrowly—passed by both the Senate and the House, and Pierce signed it into law. This started a chain of events that wouldn't end until the Civil War, a mere seven years away.

Chapter 8

Bleeding Kansas

If President Pierce had hoped that signing the Kansas-Nebraska bill would put an end to the slavery agitation, he was sadly mistaken. Even as the bill was being debated, angry antislavery Americans—Whigs and Democrats alike—were meeting in Ripon, Wisconsin, to form a new political party. Taking their name from Thomas Jefferson's original party, they called themselves the Republicans. Their battle cry was, "Repeal the Kansas-Nebraska Act. Down with slavery!" In the congressional elections of 1854, there were 15 Republican senators to 40 Democrats, while in the House the Republicans led, 108 to 83.

This was the least violent outcome of the Kansas-Nebraska Act. As soon as the Kansas Territory opened up, trouble began. Land speculators rushed in to defraud the Indians out of their lands. Armed southerners rushed in to terrorize settlers into voting for slavery. Northerners rushed in with New England money to ensure the territory would remain free. And the man President Pierce had named governor, Andrew H. Reeder of Pennsylvania, was inept at best. At worst, he was crooked, being a land speculator himself.

The Fugitive Slave Law in action

Things went from bad to worse. A February 1855 census showed 2,905 voters in Kansas. But when the election was held to set up a territorial legislature on March 30, 6,307 votes were cast. Most of these additional votes were cast by armed Missourians who had crossed the border to intimidate native settlers and ensure a proslavery vote. Their tactics worked, and a proslavery legislature was established at Shawnee, Kansas.

The antislavery settlers immediately protested and held their own election. On January 15, 1856, these "Free-Staters" elected a governor and set up their own legislature in Topeka.

Pierce recognized that the two territorial governments were headed for conflict. He tried to calm matters by giving federal support to one side—the proslavery faction in Shawnee. In Pierce's view, the original territorial legislature was the only "duly constituted" one. Then, fearing violence, he asked Congress to approve sending federal troops to Kansas to keep peace.

Now everyone was up in arms. The South was still angry at Pierce for appointing Reeder—a northerner—governor of Kansas. When Pierce removed Reeder for failure to fulfill his duties, the North turned against him. Each side felt he was unfairly favoring the other.

Things soon came to a head. On May 21, 1856, a group of armed proslavers attacked the antislavery town of Lawrence, Kansas, burning the town and killing five men. Two days before, Senator Charles Sumner of Massachusetts had denounced proslavery forces in a scathing speech. His harshest language was reserved for Senator Andrew Butler of South Carolina for his "championship of human wrongs."

On May 22, Butler's nephew, Congressman Preston Brooks, marched onto the Senate floor and physically attacked Sumner at his desk. Sumner could neither escape nor defend himself as Brooks struck at him repeatedly with his cane. In the end, Brooks stopped only when he broke his cane on the senseless Sumner.

Senator Charles Sumner of Massachusetts

News of this attack (from which it took Sumner three years to recover) only served to fan the flames of hatred. On May 24, abolitionist John Brown led an attack against a settlement on Pottawatomie Creek. Brown's gang dragged five from their beds and murdered them.

Now a civil war in Kansas had begun in earnest. Fighting broke out all over the state, and by the fall of 1856, two hundred men had been killed. Finally President Pierce had no choice. He stepped in to appoint yet another new governor, John White Geary. Geary had an abundance of federal troops at his disposal, and he did not hesitate to use them. By the middle of September, an uneasy truce had been achieved.

James Buchanan, fifteenth president of the United States

But the truce came too late to save Franklin Pierce's political fortunes, for 1856 was also an election year. When the Democratic national convention met on June 2, 1856, right in the midst of the Kansas uprisings, Pierce was considered too dangerous to put up for nomination. He started out as a candidate all right, but by the fourteenth ballot his name had been dropped. Once again, the Democrats needed a compromise candidate to put in front of the voters. Pierce simply had too many enemies to be considered a safe candidate. In the end, James Buchanan was named the Democratic nominee for president. As American ambassador to England for the past four years, Buchanan had avoided all the Kansas-Nebraska troubles. In November, voters elected Buchanan president. Franklin Pierce had now truly resigned from public life.

A cartoon on the "Dis-United States" that appeared in *Punch*, a London magazine

This cartoon shows Lady Liberty saying to Pierce: "Your time is out, you have not fulfilled my expectations. I hope James will do better."

An 1861 photograph of Franklin Pierce

Chapter 9

The Final Years

On March 3, 1857, Franklin and Jane Pierce said good-bye to a White House that had brought them precious little happiness and a great deal of grief. Pierce left Washington the way he had entered. He was still convinced that the Union was more important than factional differences and that the slavery issue was properly left to the states, not to the federal government. As history would show, his was a short-sighted view. In actual fact, the Union could *not* survive until the question of slavery was laid to rest once and for all. As the nation expanded and its population grew, the opposition between slave and free states became incompatible with the whole notion of Union. As much as anything, Pierce was blamed because he failed to stop a steady march of events that probably no man, no matter how great a statesman, could have stopped.

But for the time being, the Pierces needed to get away from national troubles. Jane had never recovered from her grief over Benjamin's death, and to ease this Franklin took her abroad. For three years they toured Europe and then returned to Concord to set up residence as private citizens.

By now President Buchanan was faring no better than Pierce had. Violence had broken out again in Kansas. If Pierce spoke out on the issues at all these days, it was to reaffirm his belief that slavery was constitutional. This position made him popular with southerners, and some suggested he run for president again in 1860. But Pierce had meant it when he said he was through with national politics. Perhaps by now he could see the writing on the wall that spelled out Civil War in capital letters.

As Republican Abraham Lincoln won the 1860 election, southern states had begun seceding from the Union. Pierce was called upon, along with other national figures, to try to mend the breach. But Pierce refused to intervene. As he saw it, what the South was doing was perfectly justifiable. The states'-rights provisions of the Constitution protected slavery, and the North had no legal right to interfere with how southern states conducted their business.

Finally and inevitably, war came. Pierce supported the Union, but he was vocal about his opposition to the war. For this, Secretary of State Seward accused him of treason. The accusation hurt deeply. Pierce's only concern, ever, had been to uphold the rights of the Union as set forth in the Constitution by the founding fathers. But despite the hurt, Pierce continued to speak out on the issues according to his conscience. When Lincoln issued his Emancipation Proclamation, Pierce concluded that the abolitionists had won and that the Constitution had been overthrown. Eventually, he alienated so many of his former friends and supporters that, even in his native New Hampshire, he was looked upon with scorn and distaste.

Above: Slaves being sold at an auction in South Carolina
Below: Lincoln presents the Emancipation Proclamation to his cabinet.

The extent of this anti-Pierce sentiment was demonstrated following Lincoln's assassination in 1865. A crowd gathered in Concord's town center and set out for the ex-president's house. When they arrived, shouting and ill-tempered, they demanded that Pierce demonstrate his Union loyalty by showing a United States flag.

Pierce, ever firm in his convictions, didn't back down before the angry crowd. "It is not necessary for me to show my devotion for the Stars and Stripes by any special exhibitions," he said. "If the period which I have served our state and country in various situations, commencing more than thirty-five years ago, has left in doubt the question of my devotion to the flag, the Constitution and the Union, it is too late now to rescue it by any such exhibition."

Abashed, the crowd melted away. But the wounds to Pierce's spirit never really healed. His last years were lonely ones. Jane died in 1863, and after her death Pierce lived in virtual seclusion. To himself, he was a man who had given his life in service to his country. To his fellow countrymen, he was a traitor, disloyal to the cause of Union. It was a bitter pill to swallow.

Franklin Pierce died in Concord on October 8, 1869, at the age of sixty-four. He is often referred to as one of the weaker of the American presidents for his failure to close the gap between North and South in the decade before the Civil War. But it is doubtful whether any man could have fared better in those years. For all his failings, Franklin Pierce was ever guided by principle, not personal gain. He owned no slaves and had nothing to gain by maintaining

Pierce's residence in Concord, New Hampshire

the legality of slavery. In his view, slavery was protected by the Constitution. And as a public servant, Pierce knew his duty to uphold the Constitution. It followed logically, then, that it was also his duty to protect slavery.

It was this stand of principle—however misguided it might seem when compared to the higher principle of the morality of slavery—that was to prove Franklin Pierce's undoing. In the end, his principles left him one of the most unhappy, and least understood, of our nation's presidents.

Above: A rare daguerreotype of President Franklin Pierce
Opposite page: Jane Means Appleton Pierce, around the year 1860

Chronology of American History

(Shaded area covers events in Franklin Pierce's lifetime.)

About A.D. 982 — Eric the Red, born in Norway, reaches Greenland in one of the first European voyages to North America.

About 1000 — Leif Ericson (Eric the Red's son) leads what is thought to be the first European expedition to mainland North America; Leif probably lands in Canada.

1492 — Christopher Columbus, seeking a sea route from Spain to the Far East, discovers the New World.

1497 — John Cabot reaches Canada in the first English voyage to North America.

1513 — Ponce de Léon explores Florida in search of the fabled Fountain of Youth.

1519-1521 — Hernando Cortés of Spain conquers Mexico.

1534 — French explorers led by Jacques Cartier enter the Gulf of St. Lawrence in Canada.

1540 — Spanish explorer Francisco Coronado begins exploring the American Southwest, seeking the riches of the mythical Seven Cities of Cibola.

1565 — St. Augustine, Florida, the first permanent European town in what is now the United States, is founded by the Spanish.

1607 — Jamestown, Virginia, is founded, the first permanent English town in the present-day U.S.

1608 — Frenchman Samuel de Champlain founds the village of Quebec, Canada.

1609 — Henry Hudson explores the eastern coast of present-day U.S. for the Netherlands; the Dutch then claim parts of New York, New Jersey, Delaware, and Connecticut and name the area New Netherland.

1619 — The English colonies' first shipment of black slaves arrives in Jamestown.

1620 — English Pilgrims found Massachusetts' first permanent town at Plymouth.

1621 — Massachusetts Pilgrims and Indians hold the famous first Thanksgiving feast in colonial America.

1623 — Colonization of New Hampshire is begun by the English.

1624 — Colonization of present-day New York State is begun by the Dutch at Fort Orange (Albany).

1625 — The Dutch start building New Amsterdam (now New York City).

1630 — The town of Boston, Massachusetts, is founded by the English Puritans.

1633 — Colonization of Connecticut is begun by the English.

1634 — Colonization of Maryland is begun by the English.

1636 — Harvard, the colonies' first college, is founded in Massachusetts. Rhode Island colonization begins when Englishman Roger Williams founds Providence.

1638 — Delaware colonization begins as Swedes build Fort Christina at present-day Wilmington.

1640 — Stephen Daye of Cambridge, Massachusetts prints *The Bay Psalm Book*, the first English-language book published in what is now the U.S.

1643 — Swedish settlers begin colonizing Pennsylvania.

About 1650 — North Carolina is colonized by Virginia settlers.

1660 — New Jersey colonization is begun by the Dutch at present-day Jersey City.

1670 — South Carolina colonization is begun by the English near Charleston.

1673 — Jacques Marquette and Louis Jolliet explore the upper Mississippi River for France.

1682—Philadelphia, Pennsylvania, is settled. La Salle explores Mississippi River all the way to its mouth in Louisiana and claims the whole Mississippi Valley for France.

1693—College of William and Mary is founded in Williamsburg, Virginia.

1700—Colonial population is about 250,000.

1703—Benjamin Franklin is born in Boston.

1732—George Washington, first president of the U.S., is born in Westmoreland County, Virginia.

1733—James Oglethorpe founds Savannah, Georgia; Georgia is established as the thirteenth colony.

1735—John Adams, second president of the U.S., is born in Braintree, Massachusetts.

1737—William Byrd founds Richmond, Virginia.

1738—British troops are sent to Georgia over border dispute with Spain.

1739—Black insurrection takes place in South Carolina.

1740—English Parliament passes act allowing naturalization of immigrants to American colonies after seven-year residence.

1743—Thomas Jefferson is born in Albemarle County, Virginia. Benjamin Franklin retires at age thirty-seven to devote himself to scientific inquiries and public service.

1744—King George's War begins; France joins war effort against England.

1745—During King George's War, France raids settlements in Maine and New York.

1747—Classes begin at Princeton College in New Jersey.

1748—The Treaty of Aix-la-Chapelle concludes King George's War.

1749—Parliament legally recognizes slavery in colonies and the inauguration of the plantation system in the South. George Washington becomes the surveyor for Culpepper County in Virginia.

1750—Thomas Walker passes through and names Cumberland Gap on his way toward Kentucky region. Colonial population is about 1,200,000.

1751—James Madison, fourth president of the U.S., is born in Port Conway, Virginia. English Parliament passes Currency Act, banning New England colonies from issuing paper money. George Washington travels to Barbados.

1752—Pennsylvania Hospital, the first general hospital in the colonies, is founded in Philadelphia. Benjamin Franklin uses a kite in a thunderstorm to demonstrate that lightning is a form of electricity.

1753—George Washington delivers command that the French withdraw from the Ohio River Valley; French disregard the demand. Colonial population is about 1,328,000.

1754—French and Indian War begins (extends to Europe as the Seven Years' War). Washington surrenders at Fort Necessity.

1755—French and Indians ambush Braddock. Washington becomes commander of Virginia troops.

1756—England declares war on France.

1758—James Monroe, fifth president of the U.S., is born in Westmoreland County, Virginia.

1759—Cherokee Indian war begins in southern colonies; hostilities extend to 1761. George Washington marries Martha Dandridge Custis.

1760—George III becomes king of England. Colonial population is about 1,600,000.

1762—England declares war on Spain.

1763—Treaty of Paris concludes the French and Indian War and the Seven Years' War. England gains Canada and most other French lands east of the Mississippi River.

1764—British pass the Sugar Act to gain tax money from the colonists. The issue of taxation without representation is first introduced in Boston. John Adams marries Abigail Smith.

1765—Stamp Act goes into effect in the colonies. Business virtually stops as almost all colonists refuse to use the stamps.

1766—British repeal the Stamp Act.

1767—John Quincy Adams, sixth president of the U.S. and son of second president John Adams, is born in Braintree, Massachusetts. Andrew Jackson, seventh president of the U.S., is born in Waxhaw settlement, South Carolina.

1769—Daniel Boone sights the Kentucky Territory.

1770—In the Boston Massacre, British soldiers kill five colonists and injure six. Townshend Acts are repealed, thus eliminating all duties on imports to the colonies except tea.

1771—Benjamin Franklin begins his autobiography, a work that he will never complete. The North Carolina assembly passes the "Bloody Act," which makes rioters guilty of treason.

1772—Samuel Adams rouses colonists to consider British threats to self-government.

1773—English Parliament passes the Tea Act. Colonists dressed as Mohawk Indians board British tea ships and toss 342 casks of tea into the water in what becomes known as the Boston Tea Party. William Henry Harrison is born in Charles City County, Virginia.

1774—British close the port of Boston to punish the city for the Boston Tea Party. First Continental Congress convenes in Philadelphia.

1775—American Revolution begins with battles of Lexington and Concord, Massachusetts. Second Continental Congress opens in Philadelphia. George Washington becomes commander-in-chief of the Continental army.

1776—Declaration of Independence is adopted on July 4.

1777—Congress adopts the American flag with thirteen stars and thirteen stripes. John Adams is sent to France to negotiate peace treaty.

1778—France declares war against Great Britain and becomes U.S. ally.

1779—British surrender to Americans at Vincennes. Thomas Jefferson is elected governor of Virginia. James Madison is elected to the Continental Congress.

1780—Benedict Arnold, first American traitor, defects to the British.

1781—Articles of Confederation go into effect. Cornwallis surrenders to George Washington at Yorktown, ending the American Revolution.

1782—American commissioners, including John Adams, sign peace treaty with British in Paris. Thomas Jefferson's wife, Martha, dies. Martin Van Buren is born in Kinderhook, New York.

1784—Zachary Taylor is born near Barboursville, Virginia.

1785—Congress adopts the dollar as the unit of currency. John Adams is made minister to Great Britain. Thomas Jefferson is appointed minister to France.

1786—Shays's Rebellion begins in Massachusetts.

1787—Constitutional Convention assembles in Philadelphia, with George Washington presiding; U.S. Constitution is adopted. Delaware, New Jersey, and Pennsylvania become states.

1788—Virginia, South Carolina, New York, Connecticut, New Hampshire, Maryland, and Massachusetts become states. U.S. Constitution is ratified. New York City is declared U.S. capital.

1789—Presidential electors elect George Washington and John Adams as first president and vice-president. Thomas Jefferson is appointed secretary of state. North Carolina becomes a state. French Revolution begins.

1790—Supreme Court meets for the first time. Rhode Island becomes a state. First national census in the U.S. counts 3,929,214 persons. John Tyler is born in Charles City County, Virginia.

1791—Vermont enters the Union. U.S. Bill of Rights, the first ten amendments to the Constitution, goes into effect. District of Columbia is established. James Buchanan is born in Stony Batter, Pennsylvania.

1792—Thomas Paine publishes *The Rights of Man*. Kentucky becomes a state. Two political parties are formed in the U.S., Federalist and Republican. Washington is elected to a second term, with Adams as vice-president.

1793—War between France and Britain begins; U.S. declares neutrality. Eli Whitney invents the cotton gin; cotton production and slave labor increase in the South.

1794—Eleventh Amendment to the Constitution is passed, limiting federal courts' power. "Whiskey Rebellion" in Pennsylvania protests federal whiskey tax. James Madison marries Dolley Payne Todd.

1795—George Washington signs the Jay Treaty with Great Britain. Treaty of San Lorenzo, between U.S. and Spain, settles Florida boundary and gives U.S. right to navigate the Mississippi. James Polk is born near Pineville, North Carolina.

1796—Tennessee enters the Union. Washington gives his Farewell Address, refusing a third presidential term. John Adams is elected president and Thomas Jefferson vice-president.

1797—Adams recommends defense measures against possible war with France. Napoleon Bonaparte and his army march against Austrians in Italy. U.S. population is about 4,900,000.

1798—Washington is named commander-in-chief of the U.S. Army. Department of the Navy is created. Alien and Sedition Acts are passed. Napoleon's troops invade Egypt and Switzerland.

1799—George Washington dies at Mount Vernon, New York. James Monroe is elected governor of Virginia. French Revolution ends. Napoleon becomes ruler of France.

1800—Thomas Jefferson and Aaron Burr tie for president. U.S. capital is moved from Philadelphia to Washington, D.C. The White House is built as presidents' home. Spain returns Louisiana to France. Millard Fillmore is born in Locke, New York.

1801—After thirty-six ballots, House of Representatives elects Thomas Jefferson president, making Burr vice-president. James Madison is named secretary of state.

1802—Congress abolishes excise taxes. U.S. Military Academy is founded at West Point, New York.

1803—Ohio enters the Union. Louisiana Purchase treaty is signed with France, greatly expanding U.S. territory.

1804—Twelfth Amendment to the Constitution rules that president and vice-president be elected separately. Alexander Hamilton is killed by Vice-President Aaron Burr in a duel. Orleans Territory is established. Napoleon crowns himself emperor of France. Franklin Pierce is born in Hillsborough Lower Village, New Hampshire.

1805—Thomas Jefferson begins his second term as president. Lewis and Clark expedition reaches the Pacific Ocean.

1806—Coinage of silver dollars is stopped; resumes in 1836.

1807—Aaron Burr is acquitted in treason trial. Embargo Act closes U.S. ports to trade.

1808—James Madison is elected president. Congress outlaws importing slaves from Africa. Andrew Johnson is born in Raleigh, North Carolina.

1809—Abraham Lincoln is born near Hodgenville, Kentucky.

1810—U.S. population is 7,240,000.

1811—William Henry Harrison defeats Indians at Tippecanoe. Monroe is named secretary of state.

1812—Louisiana becomes a state. U.S. declares war on Britain (War of 1812). James Madison is reelected president. Napoleon invades Russia.

1813—British forces take Fort Niagara and Buffalo, New York.

1814—Francis Scott Key writes "The Star-Spangled Banner." British troops burn much of Washington, D.C., including the White House. Treaty of Ghent ends War of 1812. James Monroe becomes secretary of war.

1815—Napoleon meets his final defeat at Battle of Waterloo.

1816—James Monroe is elected president. Indiana becomes a state.

1817—Mississippi becomes a state. Construction on Erie Canal begins.

1818—Illinois enters the Union. The present thirteen-stripe flag is adopted. Border between U.S. and Canada is agreed upon.

1819—Alabama becomes a state. U.S. purchases Florida from Spain. Thomas Jefferson establishes the University of Virginia.

1820—James Monroe is reelected. In the Missouri Compromise, Maine enters the Union as a free (non-slave) state.

1821—Missouri enters the Union as a slave state. Santa Fe Trail opens the American Southwest. Mexico declares independence from Spain. Napoleon Bonaparte dies.

1822—U.S. recognizes Mexico and Colombia. Liberia in Africa is founded as a home for freed slaves. Ulysses S. Grant is born in Point Pleasant, Ohio. Rutherford B. Hayes is born in Delaware, Ohio.

1823—Monroe Doctrine closes North and South America to European colonizing or invasion.

1824—House of Representatives elects John Quincy Adams president when none of the four candidates wins a majority in national election. Mexico becomes a republic.

1825—Erie Canal is opened. U.S. population is 11,300,000.

1826—Thomas Jefferson and John Adams both die on July 4, the fiftieth anniversary of the Declaration of Independence.

1828—Andrew Jackson is elected president. Tariff of Abominations is passed, cutting imports.

1829—James Madison attends Virginia's constitutional convention. Slavery is abolished in Mexico. Chester A. Arthur is born in Fairfield, Vermont.

1830—Indian Removal Act to resettle Indians west of the Mississippi is approved.

1831—James Monroe dies in New York City. James A. Garfield is born in Orange, Ohio. Cyrus McCormick develops his reaper.

1832—Andrew Jackson, nominated by the new Democratic Party, is reelected president.

1833—Britain abolishes slavery in its colonies. Benjamin Harrison is born in North Bend, Ohio.

1835—Federal government becomes debt-free for the first time.

1836—Martin Van Buren becomes president. Texas wins independence from Mexico. Arkansas joins the Union. James Madison dies at Montpelier, Virginia.

1837—Michigan enters the Union. U.S. population is 15,900,000. Grover Cleveland is born in Caldwell, New Jersey.

1840—William Henry Harrison is elected president.

1841—President Harrison dies in Washington, D.C., one month after inauguration. Vice-President John Tyler succeeds him.

1843—William McKinley is born in Niles, Ohio.

1844—James Knox Polk is elected president. Samuel Morse sends first telegraphic message.

1845—Texas and Florida become states. Potato famine in Ireland causes massive emigration from Ireland to U.S. Andrew Jackson dies near Nashville, Tennessee.

1846—Iowa enters the Union. War with Mexico begins.

1847—U.S. captures Mexico City.

1848—John Quincy Adams dies in Washington, D.C. Zachary Taylor becomes president. Treaty of Guadalupe Hidalgo ends Mexico-U.S. war. Wisconsin becomes a state.

1849—James Polk dies in Nashville, Tennessee.

1850—President Taylor dies in Washington, D.C.; Vice-President Millard Fillmore succeeds him. California enters the Union, breaking tie between slave and free states.

1852—Franklin Pierce is elected president.

1853—Gadsden Purchase transfers Mexican territory to U.S.

1854—"War for Bleeding Kansas" is fought between slave and free states.

1855—Czar Nicholas I of Russia dies, succeeded by Alexander II.

1856—James Buchanan is elected president. In Massacre of Potawatomi Creek, Kansas-slavers are murdered by free-staters. Woodrow Wilson is born in Staunton, Virginia.

1857—William Howard Taft is born in Cincinnati, Ohio.

1858—Minnesota enters the Union. Theodore Roosevelt is born in New York City.

1859—Oregon becomes a state.

94

1860—Abraham Lincoln is elected president; South Carolina secedes from the Union in protest.

1861—Arkansas, Tennessee, North Carolina, and Virginia secede. Kansas enters the Union as a free state. Civil War begins.

1862—Union forces capture Fort Henry, Roanoke Island, Fort Donelson, Jacksonville, and New Orleans; Union armies are defeated at the battles of Bull Run and Fredericksburg. Martin Van Buren dies in Kinderhook, New York. John Tyler dies near Charles City, Virginia.

1863—Lincoln issues Emancipation Proclamation: all slaves held in rebelling territories are declared free. West Virginia becomes a state.

1864—Abraham Lincoln is reelected. Nevada becomes a state.

1865—Lincoln is assassinated in Washington, D.C., and succeeded by Andrew Johnson. U.S. Civil War ends on May 26. Thirteenth Amendment abolishes slavery. Warren G. Harding is born in Blooming Grove, Ohio.

1867—Nebraska becomes a state. U.S. buys Alaska from Russia for $7,200,000. Reconstruction Acts are passed.

1868—President Johnson is impeached for violating Tenure of Office Act, but is acquitted by Senate. Ulysses S. Grant is elected president. Fourteenth Amendment prohibits voting discrimination. James Buchanan dies in Lancaster, Pennsylvania.

1869—Franklin Pierce dies in Concord, New Hampshire.

1870—Fifteenth Amendment gives blacks the right to vote.

1872—Grant is reelected over Horace Greeley. General Amnesty Act pardons ex-Confederates. Calvin Coolidge is born in Plymouth Notch, Vermont.

1874—Millard Fillmore dies in Buffalo, New York. Herbert Hoover is born in West Branch, Iowa.

1875—Andrew Johnson dies in Carter's Station, Tennessee.

1876—Colorado enters the Union. "Custer's last stand": he and his men are massacred by Sioux Indians at Little Big Horn, Montana.

1877—Rutherford B. Hayes is elected president as all disputed votes are awarded to him.

1880—James A. Garfield is elected president.

1881—President Garfield is assassinated and dies in Elberon, New Jersey. Vice-President Chester A. Arthur succeeds him.

1882—U.S. bans Chinese immigration. Franklin D. Roosevelt is born in Hyde Park, New York.

1884—Grover Cleveland is elected president. Harry S. Truman is born in Lamar, Missouri.

1885—Ulysses S. Grant dies in Mount McGregor, New York.

1886—Statue of Liberty is dedicated. Chester A. Arthur dies in New York City.

1888—Benjamin Harrison is elected president.

1889—North Dakota, South Dakota, Washington, and Montana become states.

1890—Dwight D. Eisenhower is born in Denison, Texas. Idaho and Wyoming become states.

1892—Grover Cleveland is elected president.

1893—Rutherford B. Hayes dies in Fremont, Ohio.

1896—William McKinley is elected president. Utah becomes a state.

1898—U.S. declares war on Spain over Cuba.

1900—McKinley is reelected. Boxer Rebellion against foreigners in China begins.

1901—McKinley is assassinated by anarchist Leon Czolgosz in Buffalo, New York; Theodore Roosevelt becomes president. Benjamin Harrison dies in Indianapolis, Indiana.

1902—U.S. acquires perpetual control over Panama Canal.

1903—Alaskan frontier is settled.

1904—Russian-Japanese War breaks out. Theodore Roosevelt wins presidential election.

1905 — Treaty of Portsmouth signed, ending Russian-Japanese War.

1906 — U.S. troops occupy Cuba.

1907 — President Roosevelt bars all Japanese immigration. Oklahoma enters the Union.

1908 — William Howard Taft becomes president. Grover Cleveland dies in Princeton, New Jersey. Lyndon B. Johnson is born near Stonewall, Texas.

1909 — NAACP is founded under W.E.B. DuBois

1910 — China abolishes slavery.

1911 — Chinese Revolution begins. Ronald Reagan is born in Tampico, Illinois.

1912 — Woodrow Wilson is elected president. Arizona and New Mexico become states.

1913 — Federal income tax is introduced in U.S. through the Sixteenth Amendment. Richard Nixon is born in Yorba Linda, California. Gerald Ford is born in Omaha, Nebraska.

1914 — World War I begins.

1915 — British liner *Lusitania* is sunk by German submarine.

1916 — Wilson is reelected president.

1917 — U.S. breaks diplomatic relations with Germany. Czar Nicholas of Russia abdicates as revolution begins. U.S. declares war on Austria-Hungary. John F. Kennedy is born in Brookline, Massachusetts.

1918 — Wilson proclaims "Fourteen Points" as war aims. On November 11, armistice is signed between Allies and Germany.

1919 — Eighteenth Amendment prohibits sale and manufacture of intoxicating liquors. Wilson presides over first League of Nations; wins Nobel Peace Prize. Theodore Roosevelt dies in Oyster Bay, New York.

1920 — Nineteenth Amendment (women's suffrage) is passed. Warren Harding is elected president.

1921 — Adolf Hitler's stormtroopers begin to terrorize political opponents.

1922 — Irish Free State is established. Soviet states form USSR. Benito Mussolini forms Fascist government in Italy.

1923 — President Harding dies in San Francisco, California; he is succeeded by Vice-President Calvin Coolidge.

1924 — Coolidge is elected president. Woodrow Wilson dies in Washington, D.C. James Carter is born in Plains, Georgia. George Bush is born in Milton, Massachusetts.

1925 — Hitler reorganizes Nazi Party and publishes first volume of *Mein Kampf*.

1926 — Fascist youth organizations founded in Germany and Italy. Republic of Lebanon proclaimed.

1927 — Stalin becomes Soviet dictator. Economic conference in Geneva attended by fifty-two nations.

1928 — Herbert Hoover is elected president. U.S. and many other nations sign Kellogg-Briand pacts to outlaw war.

1929 — Stock prices in New York crash on "Black Thursday"; the Great Depression begins.

1930 — Bank of U.S. and its many branches close (most significant bank failure of the year). William Howard Taft dies in Washington, D.C.

1931 — Emigration from U.S. exceeds immigration for first time as Depression deepens.

1932 — Franklin D. Roosevelt wins presidential election in a Democratic landslide.

1933 — First concentration camps are erected in Germany. U.S. recognizes USSR and resumes trade. Twenty-First Amendment repeals prohibition. Calvin Coolidge dies in Northampton, Massachusetts.

1934 — Severe dust storms hit Plains states. President Roosevelt passes U.S. Social Security Act.

1936 — Roosevelt is reelected. Spanish Civil War begins. Hitler and Mussolini form Rome-Berlin Axis.

1937 — Roosevelt signs Neutrality Act.

1938 — Roosevelt sends appeal to Hitler and Mussolini to settle European problems amicably.

1939 — Germany takes over Czechoslovakia and invades Poland, starting World War II.

1940—Roosevelt is reelected for a third term.

1941—Japan bombs Pearl Harbor, U.S. declares war on Japan. Germany and Italy declare war on U.S.; U.S. then declares war on them.

1942—Allies agree not to make separate peace treaties with the enemies. U.S. government transfers more than 100,000 Nisei (Japanese-Americans) from west coast to inland concentration camps.

1943—Allied bombings of Germany begin.

1944—Roosevelt is reelected for a fourth term. Allied forces invade Normandy on D-Day.

1945—President Franklin D. Roosevelt dies in Warm Springs, Georgia; Vice-President Harry S. Truman succeeds him. Mussolini is killed; Hitler commits suicide. Germany surrenders. U.S. drops atomic bomb on Hiroshima; Japan surrenders: end of World War II.

1946—U.N. General Assembly holds its first session in London. Peace conference of twenty-one nations is held in Paris.

1947—Peace treaties are signed in Paris. "Cold War" is in full swing.

1948—U.S. passes Marshall Plan Act, providing $17 billion in aid for Europe. U.S. recognizes new nation of Israel. India and Pakistan become free of British rule. Truman is elected president.

1949—Republic of Eire is proclaimed in Dublin. Russia blocks land route access from Western Germany to Berlin; airlift begins. U.S., France, and Britain agree to merge their zones of occupation in West Germany. Apartheid program begins in South Africa.

1950—Riots in Johannesburg, South Africa, against apartheid. North Korea invades South Korea. U.N. forces land in South Korea and recapture Seoul.

1951—Twenty-Second Amendment limits president to two terms.

1952—Dwight D. Eisenhower resigns as supreme commander in Europe and is elected president.

1953—Stalin dies; struggle for power in Russia follows. Rosenbergs are executed for espionage.

1954—U.S. and Japan sign mutual defense agreement.

1955—Blacks in Montgomery, Alabama, boycott segregated bus lines.

1956—Eisenhower is reelected president. Soviet troops march into Hungary.

1957—U.S. agrees to withdraw ground forces from Japan. Russia launches first satellite, *Sputnik.*

1958—European Common Market comes into being. Fidel Castro begins war against Batista government in Cuba.

1959—Alaska becomes the forty-ninth state. Hawaii becomes fiftieth state. Castro becomes premier of Cuba. De Gaulle is proclaimed president of the Fifth Republic of France.

1960—Historic debates between Senator John F. Kennedy and Vice-President Richard Nixon are televised. Kennedy is elected president. Brezhnev becomes president of USSR.

1961—Berlin Wall is constructed. Kennedy and Khrushchev confer in Vienna. In Bay of Pigs incident, Cubans trained by CIA attempt to overthrow Castro.

1962—U.S. military council is established in South Vietnam.

1963—Riots and beatings by police and whites mark civil rights demonstrations in Birmingham, Alabama; 30,000 troops are called out, Martin Luther King, Jr., is arrested. Freedom marchers descend on Washington, D.C., to demonstrate. President Kennedy is assassinated in Dallas, Texas; Vice-President Lyndon B. Johnson is sworn in as president.

1964—U.S. aircraft bomb North Vietnam. Johnson is elected president. Herbert Hoover dies in New York City.

1965—U.S. combat troops arrive in South Vietnam.

1966—Thousands protest U.S. policy in Vietnam. National Guard quells race riots in Chicago.

1967—Six-Day War between Israel and Arab nations.

1968—Martin Luther King, Jr., is assassinated in Memphis, Tennessee. Senator Robert Kennedy is assassinated in Los Angeles. Riots and police brutality take place at Democratic National Convention in Chicago. Richard Nixon is elected president. Czechoslovakia is invaded by Soviet troops.

1969—Dwight D. Eisenhower dies in Washington, D.C. Hundreds of thousands of people in several U.S. cities demonstrate against Vietnam War.

1970—Four Vietnam War protesters are killed by National Guardsmen at Kent State University in Ohio.

1971—Twenty-Sixth Amendment allows eighteen-year-olds to vote.

1972—Nixon visits Communist China; is reelected president in near-record landslide. Watergate affair begins when five men are arrested in the Watergate hotel complex in Washington, D.C. Nixon announces resignations of aides Haldeman, Ehrlichman, and Dean and Attorney General Kleindienst as a result of Watergate-related charges. Harry S. Truman dies in Kansas City, Missouri.

1973—Vice-President Spiro Agnew resigns; Gerald Ford is named vice-president. Vietnam peace treaty is formally approved after nineteen months of negotiations. Lyndon B. Johnson dies in San Antonio, Texas.

1974—As a result of Watergate cover-up, impeachment is considered; Nixon resigns and Ford becomes president. Ford pardons Nixon and grants limited amnesty to Vietnam War draft evaders and military deserters.

1975—U.S. civilians are evacuated from Saigon, South Vietnam, as Communist forces complete takeover of South Vietnam.

1976—U.S. celebrates its Bicentennial. James Earl Carter becomes president.

1977—Carter pardons most Vietnam draft evaders, numbering some 10,000.

1980—Ronald Reagan is elected president.

1981—President Reagan is shot in the chest in assassination attempt. Sandra Day O'Connor is appointed first woman justice of the Supreme Court.

1983—U.S. troops invade island of Grenada.

1984—Reagan is reelected president. Democratic candidate Walter Mondale's running mate, Geraldine Ferraro, is the first woman selected for vice-president by a major U.S. political party.

1985—Soviet Communist Party secretary Konstantin Chernenko dies; Mikhail Gorbachev succeeds him. U.S. and Soviet officials discuss arms control in Geneva. Reagan and Gorbachev hold summit conference in Geneva. Racial tensions accelerate in South Africa.

1986—Space shuttle *Challenger* explodes shortly after takeoff; crew of seven dies. U.S. bombs bases in Libya. Corazon Aquino defeats Ferdinand Marcos in Philippine presidential election.

1987—Iraqi missile rips the U.S. frigate *Stark* in the Persian Gulf, killing thirty-seven American sailors. Congress holds hearings to investigate sale of U.S. arms to Iran to finance Nicaraguan *contra* movement.

1988—George Bush is elected president. President Reagan and Soviet leader Gorbachev sign INF treaty, eliminating intermediate nuclear forces. Severe drought sweeps the United States.

1989—East Germany opens Berlin Wall, allowing citizens free exit. Communists lose control of governments in Poland, Romania, and Czechoslovakia. Chinese troops massacre over 1,000 pro-democracy student demonstrators in Beijing's Tiananmen Square.

1990—Iraq annexes Kuwait, provoking the threat of war. East and West Germany are reunited. The Cold War between the United States and the Soviet Union comes to a close. Several Soviet republics make moves toward independence.

1991—Backed by a coalition of members of the United Nations, U.S. troops drive Iraqis from Kuwait. Latvia, Lithuania, and Estonia withdraw from the USSR. The Soviet Union dissolves as its republics secede to form a commonwealth of free nations.

1992—U.N. forces fail to stop fighting in territories of former Yugoslavia. More than fifty people are killed and more than six hundred buildings burned in rioting in Los Angeles. U.S. unemployment reaches eight-year high. Hurricane Andrew devastates southern Florida and parts of Louisiana. International relief supplies and troops are sent to combat famine and violence in Somalia.

1993—U.S.-led forces use airplanes and missiles to attack military targets in Iraq. William Jefferson Clinton becomes the forty-second U.S. president.

Index

Page numbers in boldface indicate illustrations.

About the Author

Charnan Simon grew up reading anything she could get her hands on in Ohio, Georgia, Oregon, and Washington. She holds a B.A. in English Literature from Carleton College in Northfield, Minnesota, and an M.A. in English Literature from the University of Chicago. She worked in children's trade books after college and then went on to become the managing editor of *Cricket* magazine before beginning her career as a freelance author. Ms. Simon has written dozens of books and articles for young people and especially likes writing — and reading — history, biography, and fiction of all sorts.